NOAH'S ARK
and Other Bible Poems

by Virginia Hoppes

©2013 - 2016 Virginia Hoppes

Illustrations by
Victor Driver, Margaret Gaeddert, and "Dr. D"

Production Design
Victor Driver, Driver Studios • Edmond, OK
Margaret Gaeddert, Gaeddert Art & Design• Oklahoma City, OK

Cover Art
Margaret Gaeddert, Gaeddert Art & Design• Oklahoma City, OK

ISBN No: 978-0-9820466-7-8
ISBN-10: 0982046677

Second Printing 2016

Published by
Humor & Communication LLC
VH Books for Kids
P.O. Box 7104, Edmond, OK 73083

The World of Bible Heros

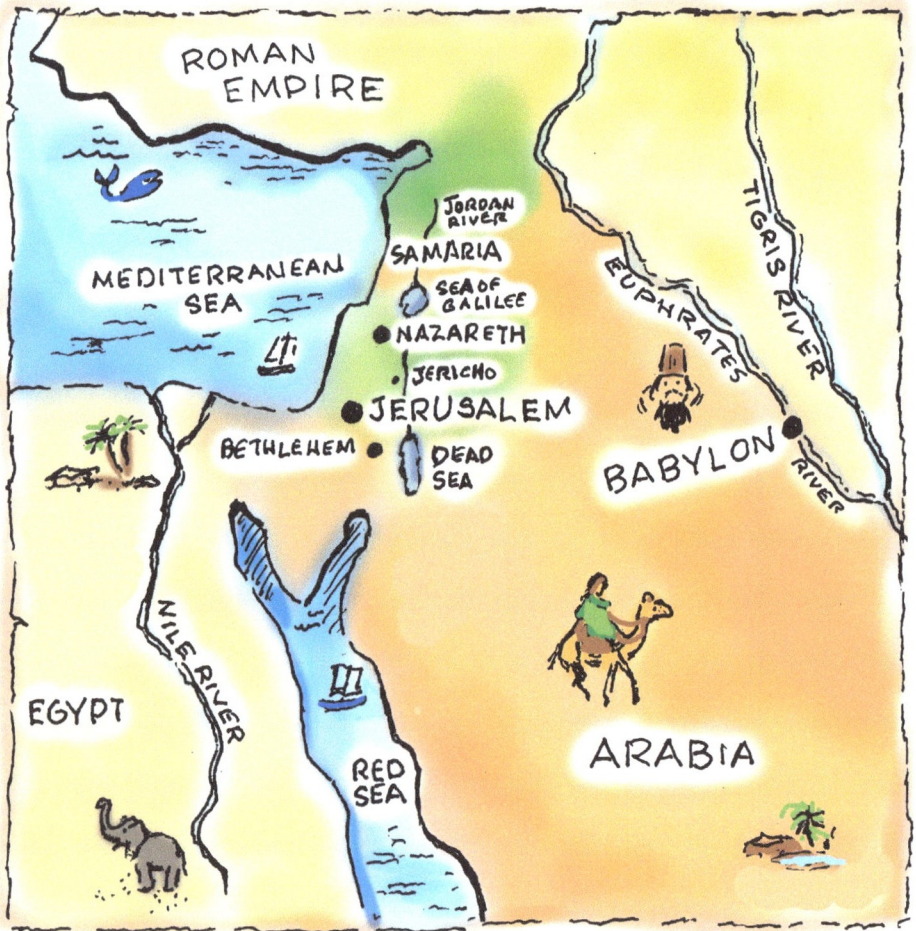

Contents

Bible verses are from the New American Standard Bible

Noah's Ark

Based on chapters 6 though 9 in Genesis

The world was once so wicked
only one good man existed.
This man, named Noah, had been working hard
for God gave him instructions
and dimensions for construction
of a boat that would be built in Noah's yard.

The neighbors watched as Noah worked.
They wondered...had he gone berserk?
Why build a boat so far from any water?
How could he ever move that ark?
It seemed he wasn't very smart
and everybody gave advice to the old codger.

But Noah wasn't bothered
about the lack of water.
He focused on his work as God commanded.
Ignoring all the criticism
Noah went about his business
and he built the boat exactly as God planned it.

And then the next thing Noah knew
the animals came, two by two,
and scampered up the ramp into the boat.
Soon Noah's family came aboard.
Though it had never rained before
the heavens opened and it poured.
Incredible! The ark began to float!

A pity that the neighbors drowned
and every living thing around.
Only those on Noah's ark survived.
Eight family members formed the crew
with an enormous job to do…
to keep the boat afloat
and keep the animals alive.

It rained for forty days and nights.
The water covered mountain heights.
The waves would toss the ship from side to side.
Yet Noah managed to control
the boat as it would rock and roll…
as scary as a roller coaster ride.

Sometimes it was a challenge
to maintain the proper balance
with the hippos and the hefty elephants.
Noah often soothed the tempers
of the lions, tigers, and leopards
and routinely cleaned the cages of the bunch.

The next one hundred fifty days
the water covered every place.
It seemed as though the rain would never stop.
However when the skies had cleared
dry areas of land appeared.
The ark was parked upon a mountain top!

The passengers aboard the ark
must wait a year to disembark
and set their feet upon the solid earth.
The world was washed and free of crime
when finally the time arrived
to step ashore and celebrate new birth.

God later promised everyone
there'd never be another flood
when every living thing would be destroyed.
A brilliant rainbow was observed,
a sign the earth would be preserved
for each new generation to enjoy.

This righteous man named Noah
was the hero God had chosen
to protect His precious creatures from extinction.
Nine hundred fifty years he lived.
What a fantastic job he did
at managing a most heroic mission!

Bible Verse: Genesis 8:22
While the earth remains, seedtime and
harvest,and cold and heat,and summer
and winter, and day and night shall
not cease.

Joseph the Dreamer

Based on Genesis, chapters 37, 41 and 42

Joseph's coat of many colors
had been made with costly dyes.
When he showed it to his brothers
he was envied…and despised.

His father, Jacob, gave this coat
to his eleventh son
who boasted he was loved the most
and was the favorite one.

Young Joseph often dreamed about
achieving wealth and fame.
Someday his family would bow down
and worship him, he claimed.

The brothers got so sick of this
conceited, cocky kid
they plotted to get rid of him
and that is what they did.

They seized him…threw him in a pit
and left him there to die.
How could they be so wicked?
The boy was terrified.

It happened that a caravan
of merchants crossed their path.
Aha! The brothers changed their plan.
They'd sell the pesky brat!
They bargained with the fellows
who immediately gave
twenty silver shekels
to buy Joseph for a slave.

The brutal brothers stripped him
of his precious coat and then
he was given to Egyptians
never to return again.

As he traveled with the traders
through the desert Joseph prayed
to be stronger, have no hatred
and no longer be afraid.

At the end of that long journey
he discovered that he'd be
working as a servant
for Egyptian royalty.

He did his job efficiently
and soon was well respected.
To live amid such luxury
was better than expected.
Since Joseph was so capable
in all his various works
he was put on Pharaoh's payroll
and had chariots for perks.

He even was requested
to interpret Pharaoh's dream…
stalks of grain…and cows…in sevens.
Half were fat and half were lean.
First, Joseph prayed, then prophesied
this dream was all about
seven good years followed by
a devastating drought.

He supervised the farmers
and advised them all to store
a part of every harvest
to be used when crops were poor.

His long-term plans were carried out.
The citizens complied.
Throughout the seven years of drought
they managed to survive.

But from surrounding countries
multitudes of people came.
These refugees were hungry…
desperate for food and grain.

By now Joseph was Governor.
He spoke before great crowds.
One day he spied his brothers
and he watched them bowing down!

They trembled and they felt ashamed
for they remembered when
they sold their brother as a slave.
Would Joseph punish them?

Might they be put in prison
or be beaten horribly?
Joseph's high position
gave him full authority.

Joseph did, in fact, forgive them
all that happened in the past.
He supplied them with provisions.
"How's my father?" Joseph asked.

The men regretted to explain
that Jacob's life was hard
because their country had no grain
and many people starved.

Jacob's tribe was then invited
to reside in Egypt where
the family reunited
and was given special care.

Though Joseph may be famous
for his fascinating coat
yet even more amazing was
compassion which he showed.

Bible Verse: Ephesians 4:32
And be kind to one another,
tenderhearted, forgiving each other,
just as God in Christ also has forgiven you.

Miriam and Baby Moses

Based on Exodus Chapter 2, verses 1-10

Miriam adored her brother
and was shocked when she discovered
the Egyptian king had made a proclamation
that every infant Hebrew son
be drowned! He said this must be done
to help reduce the foreign population.

Now Miriam was haunted
by the terrifying thought of
her baby brother drowning in the Nile.
Could someone be so wicked
he would throw a helpless infant
in the river with the snakes and crocodiles?

The baby's mother, who was smart,
had lined a basket with some tar
to make a vessel which was watertight.
She laid her baby in this boat
and prayed…then set the child afloat
while Miriam kept watching from the riverside.

The baby in the basket
drifted slowly till he landed
in the middle of some reeds and lily pads.
Along the river bank there came
the royal princess and her maids.
They waded in the water to take baths.

This princess, Pharaoh's daughter,
spied the basket in the water
and her heart was deeply touched by what she saw.
She explained to her attendants
since this baby was so precious
she'd protect him from her father's brutal law.

And as she held the infant
Miriam approached the princess
for a brilliant thought had come into her mind.
She said, "I know a lady
who would gladly nurse the baby.
She's the very nicest person you could find!"

The princess paid attention
to Miriam's suggestion
and replied, "Yes, I shall hire her right away."
The girl then brought her mother
who would tend the baby brother
in their home as usual… and be well paid!

Later, though, he must be taken
to the princess who had saved him.
She adored the child as though he were her own.
The boy enjoyed the niceties
of Egypt's high society
as well as the best education known.

The princess named him "Moses."
As a grown up he was known as
the man who saved his race from slavery.
Thank goodness that his life was spared.
Thank goodness for his mother's prayers.
Thank goodness for his sister's bravery!

Bible Verse: Exodus 2:10
She named his Moses and said,
"Because I drew him out of the water."

David and Goliath

Based on I Samuel chapter 17

David was a shepherd boy
who had a lonely job
and yet he sang sweet songs of joy
and offered praise to God.

He had a trusty slingshot
and he practiced every day
whirling it and hurling rocks
at targets far away.

His brothers had told David
about being terrified
when enemies invaded
their army camp nearby.

One opponent called Goliath
was a giant, nine feet tall!
He dared any man to fight him
and the winner would take all.

So David said, "I'll take the dare.
I'll go and fight Goliath.
I'm not scared. I've killed a bear
and once I killed a lion."

The brothers, though, objected
and they warned, "Don't fight that thug
for he could take one giant step
and crush you like a bug."

"I know," the shepherd boy replied,
"but I have the advantage
for surely God is on our side
and He and I can manage."

The Giant was obnoxious
and he didn't have a clue
what a rock in David's slingshot
and his prayers to God could do.

Goliath laughed until he shook
as he would watch the lad
pick up pebbles from the brook
and put them in a bag.

The Giant cursed and shouted threats.
His madness must be stopped!
POW! A pebble pierced his head
and he dropped dead! Ker-Plop!

Goliath's frightened army
dropped their swords and fled the camp.
The winning side would party
now that David was the champ!

Just as a shepherd guards his sheep
our God protects His people
and He is pleased if we believe
in Him…and fight what's evil.

Bible Verse: Psalms 27:1
The Lord is the strength of my life.
Of whom shall I be afraid?

King Solomon

Based on I Kings 3, verses 16-28

Solomon had prayed for wisdom
to make difficult decisions.
He was brilliant. People asked for his advice.
When citizens had problems
often Solomon would solve them.
No other man had ever been so wise.

Two women brought an infant
and each one of them insisted
that the other woman stole the child from her.
King Solomon must then decide
which one of them in fact had lied
and which of them was actually the mother.

In order to find out the truth
he said he'd split the child in two.
He showed his sword
to see what they would say.
One of the women didn't care.
To kill the boy, she thought, seemed fair
and it would end their argument that way.

The other woman screamed and cried
"My Lord, don't let my baby die.
It's better that you give the boy to *her*.
I beg that you will spare his life
for he was meant to grow and thrive.
Show mercy to this precious child, kind sir."

The king put down his sword because
he knew who the real mother was…
the one who showed her love.
The choice was clear.
He gently placed the boy, unharmed,
into the anxious mother's arms.
The guilty woman quickly disappeared.

The king ruled with intelligence
and lived amid great elegance.
He built a temple of enormous size.
Although his style was grandiose
new problems constantly arose
for Solomon had seven hundred wives!

Bible Verse: James 1:5
If any of you lacks wisdom he should ask God.

Daniel

Based on Book of Daniel, Chapters 1-6

Long ago the Babylonians
were causing pandemonium.
They occupied Jerusalem with troops.
Their king, Nebuchadnezzar,
gave the orders for the seizure
of the nation's smartest,
most outstanding youth.

So Daniel and his Hebrew friends
were captured in Jerusalem
and carried off into a foreign land.
When they were told to bow before
the golden idols they deplored
the group refused to follow the command.

The meals served to these men were wrong…
the food too rich, the wines too strong
and so a simpler diet was requested.
But guards feared if a change was made
the king might go into a rage.
And someone possibly could be beheaded!

Still Daniel wanted to be served
the type of meals his men preferred…
a diet he considered more nutritious.
His wishes seemed incredible…
just water and some vegetables…
no more wine and no exotic dishes.

A brave official held a test.
Would vegetarians fare best
or would the ones who dined on royal food?
In ten days Daniel and his friends
displayed that they had greater strength
were healthier and in a better mood.

No be headings, thankfully.
Now Daniel's men could happily
enjoy their satisfying veggie diets.
However, none of them agreed
to worship idols as decreed
so they were punished due to their defiance.

Three men with odd names faced the foe…
Shadrach, Meshach , Abednego…
all thrown into an oven's hottest flames.
And Daniel, too, faced torture
when he disobeyed the orders
and was put into the pit where lions raged.

God rescued these brave men He loved
by sending angels from above
into the blazing furnace and the lions' cage.
The fire was instantly put out.
An angel shut the lions' mouths
so Daniel and his three companions
managed to escape.

The new king, who was Darius,
had now become aware of this…
how God had saved the captives
from disaster.

The king announced a brand new law
because of miracles he saw…
The God of Daniel was to be
revered forever after.

Bible verse: Deuteronomy 31:6
The Lord your God goes with you. He will
never leave you or forsake you.

Jesus of Nazareth

The Good Samaritan

Based on Luke, chapter 10, verses 27-37

In the bible there's a quote:
"Love your neighbor as yourself."
A neighbor usually lives close
but might he come from someplace else?

A lawyer once asked Jesus,
"Who's my neighbor?" and was told
about a man who had been seized
by thieves along the road.

The bandits grabbed his money
and they whacked him on the head.
He was battered, bruised, and bloody
and abandoned there, half-dead.

A priest came by and witnessed
this poor man who moaned in pain
but the priest had other business
and refused to be detained.

A second traveler passed the spot.
He gasped and was appalled
but yet he felt he'd rather not
become involved at all.

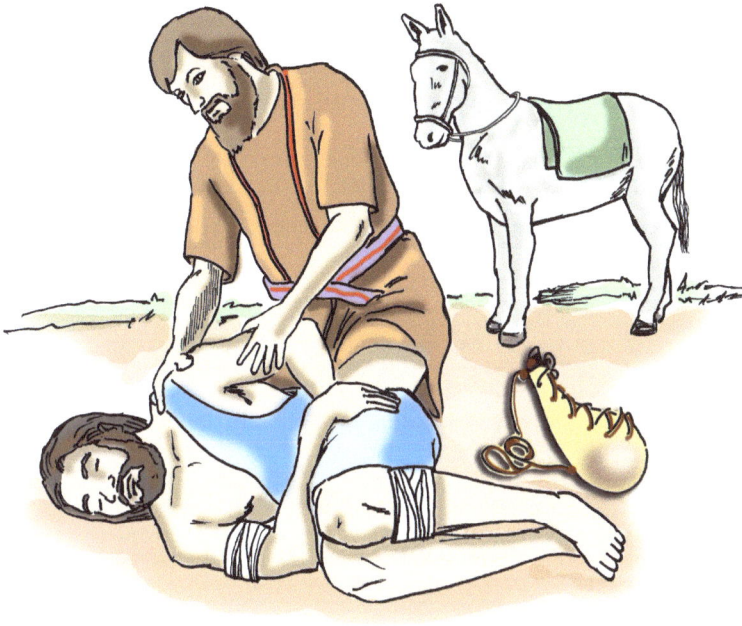

A third man, on a donkey,
traveled from Samaria,
a country which was thought
to be a hostile area.

This foreign fellow halted
and he knelt down at the side
of the man who'd been assaulted.
What help could he provide?

The stranger gave the victim
sips of water from his flask
and cleaned the wounds inflicted…
a time-consuming task.

He very gently lifted him
upon the donkey's back
and took him to the nearest inn
to rest from the attack.

At the hospice the Samaritan
then promised he would pay
the bill for care and medicine
when he returned next day.

And Jesus said, "Do likewise.
Love your neighbor as yourself."
Who's the neighbor Jesus cited?
The Samaritan who helped.

Bible verse: Luke 10:27
Love the Lord your God with all your heart
and with all your soul
and with all your strength
and with all your mind and
love your neighbor as yourself.

Zaccheus

Based on Luke, chapter 19, verses 1-10

Long ago in Jericho
excitement filled the air
as Jesus traveled down the road
and preached to people there.

A little man named Zaccheus
stood high upon his toes
for he was very anxious
to see Jesus coming close.

But Zaccheus became upset
with people who were rude.
They shoved in front of him and kept
obstructing all his view.

A sycamore tree luckily
was near the road and so
Zaccheus climbed up the tree
and watched the scene below.

When Jesus spied this little guy
perched high upon a limb
he called out, saying that he'd like
to spend some time with him.

And folks began to whisper,
"Doesn't Jesus realize
 that runt is just a chiseler
 the citizens despise?"

The people hated Zacchaeus
because he held the job
of collecting all their taxes
and he'd been accused of fraud.

How surprising he'd have Jesus
as his very special guest.
No one else would show the cheater
any kindness or respect.

Wow! Zacchaeus was so impressed
by Jesus and His love
he soon regretted and confessed
all he was guilty of.

He would repay, he promised,
four times the sum he stole
and vowed that he'd be honest
with the funds he now controlled.

He distributed his money
among people who were poor.
He was kind to everybody...
so different than before.

Jesus said that Zacchaeus
was lost and then was found.
This tax man was the happiest
philanthropist in town.

If you would visit Jericho
today you'd likely see
a famous site along the road...
a huge sycamore tree!

Bible verse: 2 Corinthians 9:7
God loves a cheerful giver.

A Child's Gift

Based on John, Chapter 6

A child was full of joy because
he now was on his way
to join the crowd where Jesus was
and hear what He would say.

His mom had lovingly prepared
a snack for him to take…
delicious fish…enough to share…
and loaves of bread she'd baked.

While listening to Jesus preach
the boy began to wonder…
might the Teacher need to eat?
It soon was time for supper.

The lad approached the leaders
of the gathering and said,
"Please give this food to Jesus…
these fish and loaves of bread."

A disciple known as Andrew
then accepted the boy's gift
and handed it to Jesus who
gave thanks to God for it.

The crowd kept watching Jesus
as they sat there on the grass.
He broke the food in pieces
and the bread and fish were passed.

An awesome miracle occurred.
The meal was multiplied!
At least six thousand people were
well-fed and satisfied.

That night the boy could hardly wait
to tell his mom about
how Jesus blessed the snack she made
and fed the hungry crowd.

Yes, miracles are possible.
The story still lives on.
It's told in all four gospels…
Matthew, Mark and Luke and John.

We, too, can give to Jesus
our love and when we try
to live the way He teaches
then *our* blessings multiply!

Bible verse: Hebrews 13:15
Do not forget to do good and to share
with others for with such sacrifices
God is pleased.

Journey to Jerusalem

Based on Luke 2, verses 41-52

Jesus, his family and his friends
took tents and camping gear
and headed for Jerusalem
for passover each year.

Jesus now was twelve years old
and soon to be a man
so he could join the menfolk
traveling in a caravan.

Or he could hike with older boys
who gathered for the trip
for they walked faster and enjoyed
great fun and fellowship.

The mothers and the youngsters
usually stayed together, too,
caring for each other
as extended families do.

It took more than a week to reach
the wondrous holy sites
where they enjoyed the festive feasts
and other sacred rites.

The Temple was magnificent...
a golden altar, marble floors
silver tables, lamps and chests
and beautifully carved doors.

Yet Jesus was more focused
on the teachers and the scribes...
so engrossed he didn't notice
that the days were flying by.

His family left Jerusalem
when someone realized
that Jesus wasn't with them!
Oh no! He'd been left behind!

Frantically, they hurried back
to search the temple grounds.
"Why were you worried?" Jesus asked
"I'm in my Father's house."

The parents watched and were amazed
to see their Son take part
in conversations and debates
with priests and patriarchs.

These men of great distinction
were astonished to behold
the knowledge and the wisdom
of this brilliant twelve-year-old.

Then Jesus went obediently
back to his school and work.
He knew his true identity...
God's Son who'd come to Earth.

Bible verse: Luke 2:51
And Jesus kept increasing in wisdom
and stature, and in favor with God and man.

The Woman at the Well

Based on John 4 verses 1-42

Jacob (Joseph's father)
dug a well and it produced
a steady flow of water
for Samaritans to use .

One day a woman came there
and it happened that she met
a fascinating stranger...
Jesus Christ from Nazareth.

Men from other places didn't
socialize at all
among the local women
if they followed protocol.

Jesus, though, had a discussion
and incredibly He knew
this woman had five husbands
plus another lover, too.

When He spoke of "living water"
she was puzzled by His words.
Was this a gift He offered
which could somehow quench her thirst?

She had heard a prophesy
that a Savior soon would come!
Could this stranger possibly
be the expected one?

The stranger brought good news, He said...
His promises seemed true.
She ran to gather all her friends
to hear His message, too.

A crowd of people listened
and for two days Jesus spoke
with extraordinary wisdom
about heaven...about hope.

The group of friends and neighbors
were inspired by what He said.
They began to call him "Savior".
Christianity soon spread.

The woman then decided
what "living water" was...
God's love and power and guidance
which He offers each of us.

The woman followed Jesus
and her faith has brought her fame.
A shame that no one seems to
know the woman's name!

Bible verse: John 3:16
For God so loved the world that He gave
his one and only son, that whoever
believes in Him shall not perish but
have eternal life.

Our Bible Heros

We hope you enjoy
these stories!
Virgina
Dr. D
Victor
Margaret

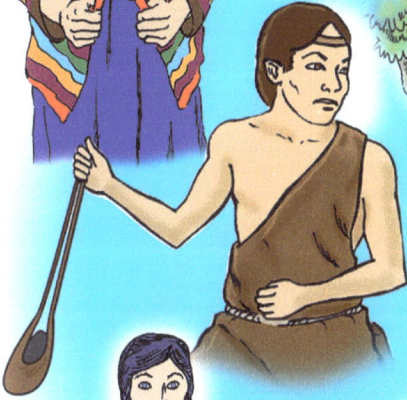

www.ingramcontent.com/pod-product-compliance
Lightning Source LLC
Chambersburg PA
CBHW041755050426
42443CB00023B/6